CW00958582

Thomas & Bray's
# STILLWATER
## FLY
# SWOTTER

Thomas & Bray's
# STILLWATER
# FLY
# SWOTTER

SWAN·HILL
PRESS

Copyright © 1998 G. R. Thomas and N. J. Bray

First published in the UK in 1998
by Swan Hill Press, an imprint of Airlife Publishing Ltd

**British Library Cataloguing-in-Publication Data**
A catalogue record for this book
is available from the British Library

ISBN 1 85310 907 X

Typeset by Servis Filmsetting Ltd
Printed in Hong Kong

**Swan Hill Press**
an imprint of Airlife Publishing Ltd
101 Longden Road, Shrewsbury, SY3 9EB, England

# Contents

# Introduction

The idea for this bankside reference book originally came from a computer program designed for personal use. The project was to produce a database that, given a set of conditions and statistics, would print out a list of fly patterns most likely to succeed on the day in question, plus tips on how to fish them. It was intended to encourage some confidence in flies other than a few old favourites.

It soon became apparent that the variables involved – the season, the prevailing weather, the weather that day and other conditions – would make the work complicated and almost impossible unless the computer went fishing too, because, somehow, it would have to allow for observations on the bank, like rises to unknown insects, muddy water or the presence of algae. So this book was born. The databases were printed out in tables, the variables became cross-references and the whole thing became much easier to use! And because it reminded us of one of those old school books crammed with exam notes, we've called it a swotter.

# A guide to fly selection

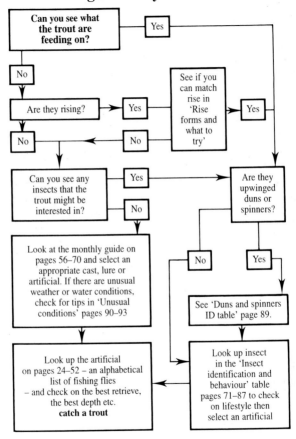

**Can you see what the trout are feeding on?** → Yes

No ↓

Are they rising? → Yes → See if you can match rise in 'Rise forms and what to try' → Yes

No ↓ ← No

Can you see any insects that the trout might be interested in? → Yes → Are they upwinged duns or spinners?

No ↓

Look at the monthly guide on pages 56–70 and select an appropriate cast, lure or artificial. If there are unusual weather or water conditions, check for tips in 'Unusual conditions' pages 90–93

No ← → Yes

See 'Duns and spinners ID table' page 89.

Look up the artificial on pages 24–52 – an alphabetical list of fishing flies – and check on the best retrieve, the best depth etc. **catch a trout**

Look up insect in the 'Insect identification and behaviour' table pages 71–87 to check on lifestyle then select an artificial

# How to use this book

Although intended as an *aide-mémoire* when conditions are unusual or when there is no activity and all familiar ruses have failed, this book is useful for the beginner too.

'Rise forms and what to try' helps identify food to which fish are rising. Pages 24–52 contain a table of 'Flies and lures', listed alphabetically, showing hook sizes, colours, and times during the season when they are at their most deadly. For example:

| Pattern<br>Wet or Dry | Colour | Best<br>Retrieve | Best<br>Depth | Best<br>Month |
|---|---|---|---|---|
| **Shrimper (Leaded)**<br>**(W)**<br>Hook Size 10–14 | Olive brown with PVC back & buff hackle | Very slow pulls with pauses | On bottom in shallow water | Gen |
| **Method-Tip** — Best early when cold: try on long leader near weeds and inflows / outflows. Watch for gentle takes as it sinks. | | | | |

Each of the eighty entries in the table describes a well-known fly or lure and there are spaces for you to add your own favourites.

If the angler is unable to make direct observations of the trout's feeding methods, the 'Best Retrieve' and 'Best Depth' suggestions help show where and how the fly is usually most successful.

Pages 71–87 contain tables, charts and information that refer to the choice of fly to be used. Pages 56–69 are a 'Monthly guide' to what insects are available to the trout, the best colours to try, and a list of imitative patterns, lures and casts to match the naturals. If only a quick reminder is required, there is an 'At-a-glance insect availability table' on page 70.

Once you have decided which fly might tempt a fish, look it up in the 'Flies and lures' table for tips on retrieve etc. Or look in 'Insect identification and behaviour', pages 71–87, to learn about the lifestyle of the insect it imitates. For example:

| Insect/Length | Month | Colours | Wing No. | Wing Colours | Tail No. |
|---|---|---|---|---|---|
| **Alder Larva**<br><br>c 20mm | Mar<br>Apr<br>May<br>and<br>Jun | Buff head and thorax with tapered brown abdomen | – | – | – |

| Movement/Depth | Flies |
|---|---|
| Crawls on bottom towards shore to pupate and hatch (adult rarely of use because it does not fall onto water in any great numbers). | Alder Larva<br>Ombudsman |

Because of the difficulty differentiating between upwinged duns, on page 89 there is a chart to help called the 'Dun Identification Table'.

These tables are followed by sections containing various tips and information likely to be of use on the bank of a stillwater.

'Unusual conditions' deals with difficult weather and water conditions and suggests ways of overcoming them.

'Where to fish' contains information and tips on how to find fish or the areas in which trout tend to shoal.

That is followed by 'General information' – tips on boat fishing, safety and many other topics.

# Rise forms and what to try

The object of this section is to suggest what the trout may be feeding on from observations of the type of rise or disturbances they make in the water. This, of course, can only be a rough guide and the angler should seek other indications to justify the selection of a fly, like identifying the type of insect hatching or falling on the surface.

Following each rise description there is a list of insects most likely to be the cause. These are listed under times of the year and the position in the list suggests the likelihood, i.e. the insect most probably the cause is at the top of the list.

## The boil

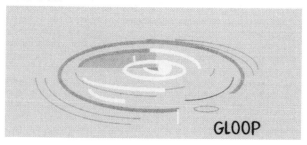

GLOOP

Caused by a fish turning quickly, the boil is a common rise to nymphs taken beneath the surface. The profile of the disturbance in the unbroken water is an indication of the depth at which the trout is feeding, e.g. the higher the ripple, the higher the fish.

# Menu

## *April*

Black or small green midge pupae

## *May*

| | |
|---|---|
| Early mornings and late afternoons | Black midge pupae<br>Small green midge pupae<br>Orange midge pupae |
| Daytime | Lake olive nymph<br>Claret nymph<br>Mayfly nymph (late May) |

## *June*

| | |
|---|---|
| Early and late | Small green, brown<br>or orange midge pupae |
| Daytime | Lake olive nymph<br>Damsel nymph<br>Caenis nymph<br>Sedge pupae<br>Claret nymph<br>Pond olive nymph<br>Mayfly nymph (1st week) |

## *July and August*

| | |
|---|---|
| Early and late | Large and small green midge<br>Red midge pupae<br>Black midge pupae<br>Small brown midge |

Daytime

Caenis nymph
Cream or orange sedge pupae
Damsel nymph
Pond olive nymph
Fry
Snails

*September and October*

Small green midge pupae
Black midge pupae
Brown midge pupae
Fry
Brown sedge pupae
Lake olive pupae
Pond olive pupae

## The head and tail

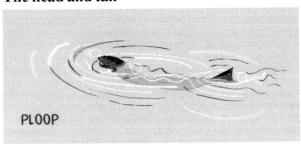

PLOOP

Trout are often observed slowly head and tailing in a straight line as they feed on a plentiful and sometimes captive supply of spent, hatching or dead flies trapped in the surface film. Cast to estimated position of next rise.

## Menu

### *April*

Hatching black or small
green midge pupae

Hawthorn fly (more of a swirl)
Spent sepia spinners

### *May*

| | |
|---|---|
| Early mornings and late afternoons | Hatching black, orange or small green midge pupae |
| Daytime | Spent lake olive or claret spinners Hawthorn fly (more of a swirl) |

### *June*

| | |
|---|---|
| Early and late | Hatching small green, brown or orange midge |
| Daytime | Lake olive, pond olive or claret spinners Flying ants |

*July and August*

Early and late             Large and small green, red,
black or small brown hatching
midge

Daytime                   Pond olive (apricot) spinner
Flying ants
Snails

*September and October*

Small green, black or
brown hatching midge pupae

Lake olive or
pond olive (apricot) spinner

## The surface-breaker

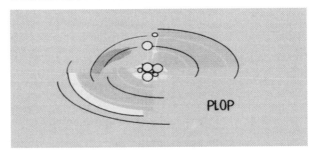

PLOP

A rise to food in or on the top, the surface-breaker is one of the most common rises. Its relative gentleness rules out some of the trout's more challenging snacks, like skittering sedge flies or exciting mayflies, and suggests a more leisurely lunch of medium-sized hatching or trapped flies.

Because the insects are on the surface, they should be easier to identify, but when consulting the list that follows, bear in mind that the fish could be taking the hatching nymph, the dun or the spinner.

### Menu

*April*

Black or small green midge

*May*

| | |
|---|---|
| Early mornings and late afternoons | Black, orange or small green midge |
| Daytime | Lake olive or claret dun/spinner |

*June*

| | |
|---|---|
| Early and late | Small green, brown or orange midge |
| Daytime | Lake olive, pond olive, or claret dun/spinner Flying ants |

*July and August*

| | |
|---|---|
| Early and late | Large and small green, black, red or small brown midge |

| Daytime | Blue winged or pond olive |
| | Dun/spinner |
| | Snails |
| | Flying ants |

*September and October*

Small green, black, brown midge
Lake olive, pond olive dun/spinner

## The slash

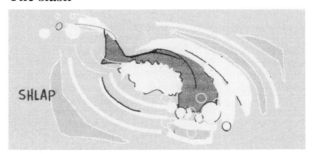

SHLAP

This violent swirling slash sends spray into the air and is usually made to large insects or those that move quickly, so displaying the potential to escape. Often the prey is knocked under the surface before being taken and it can be important that the angler pauses briefly before striking.

**Menu**

*April and May*

Hawthorn
Mayfly (Late May)

*June and July*

Mayfly (1st week)
Sedge
Damsel nymph (just under
surface)

*August, September and October*

Sedge, fry or
Daddy long legs

## The kiss

SHLURP

The leisurely kiss or sip hardly disturbs the water and suggests the fish is sucking in small insects unlikely to escape,

like spinners and newly hatched duns or hatching midge. Usually, if there is a succession of rises in a straight line, the target is caenis (see caenis in 'Insect identification and behaviour' for suggestions).

## Menu

### *April*

Black or small green hatching midge

### *May*

| | |
|---|---|
| Early mornings and late afternoons | Black, small green or orange hatching midge |
| Daytime | Lake olive or claret duns or spinners |

### *June*

| | |
|---|---|
| Early and late | Small green, brown or orange hatching midge |
| Daytime | Lake olive, claret or pond olive dun/spinner Caenis |

### *July and August*

| | |
|---|---|
| Early and late | Red, black, small brown, large and small green hatching midge |

| Daytime | Caenis |
|---|---|
| | Pond olive dun/spinner |
| | Small snails |

*September and October*

Small green, black
or brown midge

Lake olive or
pond olive duns/spinners

## The arching leap

The arching leap is a variation of *The Slash* technique for dealing with large fast-moving prey on the surface. A series of these arching rises usually means the fish are chasing skittering sedge as they struggle to become airborne. For the angler this violent splashing rise is preferable because any take is more assured.

## Menu

*April and May*

Hawthorn
Mayfly (Late May)

*June and July*

Mayfly (1st week)
Sedge
Damsel nymph (just under
surface)

*August, September and October*

Sedge or fry
Daddy long legs

# The bow wave

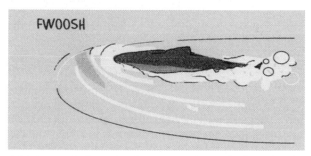

FWOOSH

A high-speed chase that leaves a wake as the fish ploughs
through the water, the bow wave is usually seen at the end

of the fishing season when trout, including large browns, venture into the shallows to gorge on minnows, stickle-backs and other fry. Sometimes it can also be merely a display of some type. An appropriate lure will catch those feeding but those involved in what may be some sort of courtship ritual rarely respond to the bait. Usually there is only fry on the menu.

## Other indications

*Deep bodied slurping*

Usually an indication that the trout is feeding on spent sedge.

*Swimming open mouthed in surface*

This is done when food supply is abundant. It may mean there are a great deal of hatching sedge or midge etc. Or the fish may be feeding on caenis or, early in the day, even daphnia.

# Flies and lures

The patterns are listed in alphabetical order. Each entry in the table holds a brief description of the fly or lure.

| | |
|---|---|
| **Pattern wet or dry** | Shows the name and whether it is usually used used wet or dry. |
| **Colours** | Shown in the first column. |
| **Best Retrieve** | Recommends the most successful retrieve, but observations on the bank may prove more valuable when deciding how to fish. |
| **Best Depth** | As above, this is a recommendation only and the angler should try different depths if it proves unsuccessful and there are no other clues to the location of the fish. |
| **Best Month** | Shows the times when the fly or lure usually proves most deadly. |
| **Methods-Tips** | Indicate any special successful uses or times etc. that the angler might find useful. |
| **Hook Size** | Hook sizes are shown above picture. |

**Spaces** have been left in and at the end of the table for you to enter the details of your favourite flies.

| Colour | Best Retrieve | Best Depth | Best Month | Pattern Wet or dry |
|--------|---------------|------------|------------|---------------------|
| Black with bronze wing | Fish with frequent pauses | Deep | Apr May June | **Ace of Spades (W)** <br> Hook Size 6–12 |
| **Method-Tip** — General black lure: try early part of season. | | | | |
| Green orange black or grey | Dap or draw through surface making wake | Surface | Gen | **Adult Midge (W) Buzzer** <br> Hook Size 12 or 14 |
| **Method-Tip** — Fish on point of long leader when trout rising to midge flying slowly over surface trailing legs in water. | | | | |
| Brown & buff | Inch very slowly | On bottom | Mar, Apr May to mid June. Try Sept & Oct | **Alder Larva (W)** <br> Hook Size 10 or 12 |
| **Method-Tip** — Fish on floating line with long leader. Watch for take as it sinks. On small waters cast to deepest parts. Late in season try early in morning or just before dark. | | | | |

| Pattern<br>Wet or Dry | Colour | Best<br>Retrieve | Best<br>Depth | Best<br>Month |
|---|---|---|---|---|
| **Amber Nymph (W)**<br>Hook Size 10–13 | Amber &<br>brown<br>with<br>honey<br>hackle | Not too<br>fast | Any, but<br>good<br>near<br>surface | Gen |
| **Method-Tip** — General fly but imitates sedge pupae – large patterns better early part of year (Apr to Jun), smaller later. Good in shallows or from boat in evenings. | | | | |
| **Appetizer (W)**<br>Hook Size 6 or 8 | White<br>body &<br>wing<br>with<br>orange<br>& silver | Medium<br>pace<br>with<br>frequent<br>pauses | Deep<br>or near<br>surface | Sept<br>Oct<br>but<br>Gen |
| **Method-Tip** — Lure: fry imitation but a general attractor. Watch for takes as it sinks. | | | | |
| **Autumn Dun (D)**<br>Hook Size 10–14 | Brown<br>with<br>gold<br>rib &<br>red<br>hackle | Tweek | Surface | Gen |
| **Method-Tip** — Imitates newly hatched dun. Cast to rise. | | | | |

| Colour | Best Retrieve | Best Depth | Best Month | Pattern Wet or dry |
|---|---|---|---|---|
| Chrome body with light red hackle | Slow-sink & draw | Any | Aug Sept Oct but Gen | **Aylott's Orange (W)** Hook Size 12 or 14 |
| **Method-Tip** — Lure: good when water coloured or heavy algae in hot weather. Use to imitate emerging sedge pupa. | | | | |
| Usually white. Can be pink etc. | Slow med | Any | Gen | **Baby Doll (W)** Hook Size 10 |
| **Method-Tip** — All round lure: any depth or retrieve or time. Try deep on sinking line when light poor and nothing moving. | | | | |
| White & silver rib red behind head & badger hen hackle | Steady pulls | Near surface or deep | Gen but try July Aug Sept | **Badger Matuka (W)** Hook Size 6 or 8 |
| **Method-Tip** — This lure swims straight. Good fry imitation. Try deep for brown trout. | | | | |

| Pattern Wet or Dry | Colour | Best Retrieve | Best Depth | Best Month |
|---|---|---|---|---|
| **Black Bear's Hair (W)** Hook Size 8 or 10 | Silver & black | Long slow or medium with frequent pauses | Deep early in day: just under surface later | Gen |
| **Method-Tip** — All round lure: try fast just below surface in late summer. | | | | |
| **Black Chenille (W)** Hook Size 8 | Black | Long steady pulls | Deep | Gen |
| **Method-Tip** — Lure. | | | | |
| **Black Ghost (W)** Hook Size 6 or 8 | Black with white wing and yellow throat | Allow slow sink then draw medium fast | Deep | Gen |
| **Method-Tip** — Successful lure said to attract brown trout. | | | | |

| Colour | Best Retrieve | Best Depth | Best Month | Pattern Wet or dry |
|--------|---------------|------------|------------|--------------------|
| Orange gold black | Jerky med-fast | Along or near bottom | Gen | **Black & Orange Marabou (W)** Hook Size 8 |
| **Method-Tip** — Lure: should be worked constantly to move marabou. | | | | |
| Black & bronze | Slow-sink & draw or on surface | Any | Gen | **Black & Peacock Spider (D or W)** Hook Size 8–12 |
| **Method-Tip** — Try during rise when trout head and tail very slowly 2 to 6 inches below surface, or when feeding on beetles or (Jun–Aug) snails. Also try dry when land beetles blown on to water. | | | | |
| Black with gold ribs & pheasant tail | Slow | Any | Gen | **Black Pennel (D)** Hook Size 10–12 |
| **Method-Tip** — Fish on a floating line when black midge or any black fly around. | | | | |

| Pattern<br>Wet or Dry | Colour | Best<br>Retrieve | Best<br>Depth | Best<br>Month |
|---|---|---|---|---|
| **Black Zulu (W)**<br>Hook Size 10–14<br> | Black with silver rib & red tag on tail | Slow or dribble on surface | Bottom (close to weeds) *or* in surface | Mar<br>Apr<br>May |
| **Method-Tip** — Emulates aquatic beetles – also good for drift fishing. | | | | |
| **Blae & Black (W)**<br>Hook Size 12–16 | Black | Med-slow | Dribble along surface or just under | Mar<br>Apr<br>May |
| **Method-Tip** — Also called duck fly – imitates emerging midge pupae/dark buzzers. | | | | |
| **Butcher (W)**<br>Hook Size 10–12 | Black with silver body & red tail | Slow on top or med-slow deep | Just under surface or deep | Mar<br>Apr<br>May<br>June |
| **Method-Tip** — General but emulates orange and silver midge – fish small and deep during day, nearer surface morning or evening. | | | | |

| Colour | Best Retrieve | Best Depth | Best Month | Pattern Wet or dry |
|--------|---------------|------------|------------|--------------------|
| **Buzzer** *See* **Midge Pupa** | | | | |
| Beige with black hackle | Inch | Crawl along bottom | Gen but best Apr–June | **Caddis Fly (W)** <br> Hook Size 10–12 |
| **Method-Tip** — Where possible use floating line with long leader. | | | | |
| Fluorescent lime green tail & wing of white marabou | Med with pauses | Any | Gen | **Cat's Whisker (W)** <br> Hook Size 6 |
| **Method-Tip** — This brightly coloured lure is a good all-rounder, but try it on grey, blustery days. Often fish are tempted into chasing it up from the bed of the lake. | | | | |
| Amber or white or olive and brown | Jerk slowly deep or, if hot, sink & draw | Any | Gen | **Chomper (W)** <br> Hook Size 10 or 12 |
| **Method-Tip** — Imitates shrimp-corixa-lice (slow on bottom) and sedge larva. Watch leader for take. Try when bright and calm if nothing moving. | | | | |

| Pattern<br>Wet or Dry | Colour | Best Retrieve | Best Depth | Best Month |
|---|---|---|---|---|
| **Church Fry (W)**<br>Hook Size 6–10<br> | Orange with red hackle & grey wing | Any (Jerky) | Any | Gen |
| | **Method-Tip** — Lure: emulates perch fry but will take fish anyway. | | | |
| **Coachman (W)**<br>Hook Size 10–14<br> | Bronze peacock with red-brown hackle and white swan wing | Sink & draw | Any | Gen |
| | **Method-Tip** — General lure but useful when it is hot & sunny and trout seem unwilling to move or feed. Try all depths. Also, if desperate during caenis rise, draw steadily through fish just below surface. | | | |
| **Coch-Y-Bonddu (W)**<br>Hook Size 8–12<br> | Peacock hurl & furnace hackle | Med-slow | Under surface or on sinking line deep | June best but gen |
| | **Method-Tip** — Good all rounder, but where there is bracken and fern this fly emulates a beetle commonly blown onto the water. | | | |

| Colour | Best Retrieve | Best Depth | Best Month | Pattern Wet or dry |
|--------|--------------|-----------|-----------|-------------------|
| Olive or brown | Slow | Deep in shallow water near weeds | Gen | **Collyer's Green & Brown Nymphs (W)**<br>Hook Size 10–12 |
| **Method-Tip** — Represents many nymphs: use floating line with long leader. Watch for gentle takes. | | | |  |
| White body with brown back | Jerk slowly sink & draw, or fast | Any | Mid July to Sept | **Corixa (W)**<br>Hook Size 10 or 12 |
| **Method-Tip** — Sink and draw a weighted fly during day or retrieve unweighted version faster just under surface in early morning or late evening or when light poor and trout chase prey into shallows. | | | | |
| White with brown back | Jerk slowly (draw and sink) | Buoyant so use sinking line | Gen | **Corixa-Plastazote (W)**<br>Hook Size 10 or 12 |
| **Method-Tip** — Floats on or near surface depending on depth and leader length – on sinking line it dives as retrieve commences. | | | |  |

| Pattern<br>Wet or Dry | Colour | Best<br>Retrieve | Best<br>Depth | Best<br>Month |
|---|---|---|---|---|
| **Daddy Long Legs –<br>Crane Fly (D)**<br>Hook Size 10 or 12 | Brown<br>with light<br>ginger<br>hackle | Dap or<br>leave still<br>with occ.<br>twitch | Top | July<br>Aug<br>Sept |
| | **Method-Tip** — Usually cast to rising trout and left – dapping can work but leave time before striking. Often good on hot still afternoons to tempt fish. Try after showers when insects brought down. | | | |
| **Damsel Nymph (&<br>Wiggle Nymph) (W)**<br>Hook Size 8–12 | Green | (A)<br>Slow | (A) On<br>bottom | (A)<br>Apr<br>May<br>June |
| | **Method-Tip** — (A). Early summer immature nymphs move awkwardly among weed on lake bed – use smaller hook. | | | |
| **(Lifecycle of<br>Nymph = 2 stages)** | (with<br>brown<br>wing<br>case) | (B)<br>Long<br>steady<br>pulls | (B) Just<br>under<br>surface | (B)<br>June<br>July<br>Aug |
| | **Method-Tip** — (B). Later they ascend to just under the surface where they swim to the shore. | | | |

| Colour | Best Retrieve | Best Depth | Best Month | Pattern Wet or dry |
|--------|---------------|------------|------------|---------------------|
| Various colours | Vary with jerks | Any | Gen | **Dog Nobbler (W)** Hook Size 6–10 |
| **Method-Tip** — Deadly lure trout cannot seem to resist. Chop back to show off marabou. | | | | |
| Gold orange brown | Slow-med | Any | Aug Sept Oct | **Dunkeld (W)** Hook Size 10–12 |
| **Method-Tip** — Small fry imitator but also generally successful. | | | | |
| Black and white with peacock head | Cast to fish, leave for 2 secs then even pull | Just below surface | Gen | **Footballer (W)** Hook Size 10–18 |
| **Method-Tip** — Represents midge pupae and designed to enter water quickly during midge rise. Fish on leader greased to within 6 in (15 cm) of the fly. If not taken immediately cast to another rise. Watch for takes as it sinks. | | | | |

| Pattern<br>Wet or Dry | Colour | Best<br>Retrieve | Best<br>Depth | Best<br>Month |
|---|---|---|---|---|
| **G & H Sedge (D)**<br>Hook Size 8–12 | Deer hair with green belly | 1) Tweek as trout pass<br>2) Dribble on top | Surface | June July Aug Sept Oct |
|  | **Method-Tip** — 1) Fish on point of a long leader and cast to path of rising trout then leave still. If not taken, try twitching line.<br>2) Dribble on top to provoke rise, especially if weather bad. | | | |
| **Gold Ribbed Hare's Ear (W or D)**<br>Hook Size 10–12 | Buff with gold rib | Slow | Any | Gen |
|  | **Method-Tip** — Fish suitable size weighted or unweighted to emulate most nymphs. | | | |
| **Greenwell's Glory (W or D)**<br>Hook Size 12–14 | Yellow green and furnace cock | Gentle dribble or slow (wet) | Wet at various depths | Gen |
| | **Method-Tip** — Represents olive dun or nymphs but a general pattern. Use wet when any olive nymphs observed. Leave in surface film to emulate spent olive spinner. | | | |

| Colour | Best Retrieve | Best Depth | Best Month | Pattern Wet or dry |
|--------|---------------|------------|------------|--------------------|
| Orange & gold | Slow | Any | Gen but best Aug Sept Oct | **Grenadier (W or D)** Hook Size 13 |
| **Method-Tip** — General pattern – sometimes used semi-dry: try slow and deep on summer days when nothing moving. | | | | |
| Grey | Slow | Just under or on surface | Gen, but best in June July | **Grey Duster (W or D)** Hook Size 12–15 |
| **Method-Tip** — General pattern – try in evenings in surface film when trout are dimpling on unknown food or caenis hatch expected. Said to induce rise. If repeatedly unsuccessful see *Caenis Nymph* in Insect Identification Table. | | | | |
| Black | None unless sinks then slow | Surface | Apr May | **Hawthorn Fly (W or D)** Hook Size 12 |
| **Method-Tip** — When natural fly blown onto water, keep back and down. Cast out gently (don't lash water). Allow to lie still. If it sinks, let it and watch line for take. Try 2 flies: one very buoyant and one on the point in surface. | | | | |

| Pattern<br>Wet or Dry | Colour | Best Retrieve | Best Depth | Best Month |
|---|---|---|---|---|
| **Invicta (W)**<br>Hook Size 10–14<br>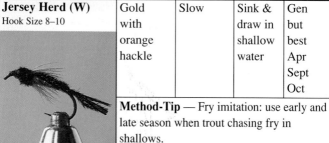 | Yellow brown gold & brown hackle | Med | Best just below or dribble on top | June<br>July<br>Aug<br>Sept<br>Oct |
| **Method-Tip** — Fair copy of hatching sedge but good general pattern fished at any depth. | | | | |
| **Jack Frost (W)**<br>Hook Size 6–10 | White body & wing with red hackle | Slow with pauses | Any | Sept<br>Oct |
| **Method-Tip** — Fry imitation. | | | | |
| **Jersey Herd (W)**<br>Hook Size 8–10 | Gold with orange hackle | Slow | Sink & draw in shallow water | Gen but best Apr Sept Oct |
| **Method-Tip** — Fry imitation: use early and late season when trout chasing fry in shallows. | | | | |

| Colour | Best Retrieve | Best Depth | Best Month | Pattern Wet or dry |
|---|---|---|---|---|
| Grey-brown with blue hackle | Dry: cast and leave | Surface | Gen | **Lake Olive (W or D)** Hook Size 10–14 |
| **Method-Tip** — Hatches are often in middle of day and sparse, but if good, cast dry to rising fish – usually in shallows – or leave to attract attention. If no luck, emulate hatching nymph with wet fly just below surface. | | | | |
| Pale buff grey with honey hackle | Cast & leave | Surface | June July Aug | **Last Hope (D)** Hook Size 17 or 18 |
| **Method-Tip** — Cast to fish rising on well-greased leader. If fails see *Caenis Nymph* in Insect Identification Table. | | | | |
| Green sepia & brown hackle | Steady pulls | 2–3ft up to surface | June July Sept | **Longhorns (W)** Hook Size 10–12 |
| **Method-Tip** — Imitates sedge pupae hatching to adult. | | | | |

| Pattern<br>Wet or Dry | Colour | Best<br>Retrieve | Best<br>Depth | Best<br>Month |
|---|---|---|---|---|
| **Mallard & Claret (W)**<br>Hook Size 10–14<br> | Dark claret with bronze speck'd wing | Slow | Any | Gen |
| **Method-Tip** — Try when uncertain what trout are feeding on: smaller sizes better early in year – large from July. | | | | |
| **Mayfly Nymph (Walker's) (W)**<br>Hook Size 8<br> | Yellow buff body with pheasant hurl thorax | Slow on lake bed & steady to surface | Any | May<br>June |
| **Method-Tip** — Use floating line with long leader. Lives in lake bed but rises directly and quickly to surface to hatch. Can also be used all through season as a large nymph lure inched along bottom (esp. on small waters). | | | | |
| **Mayfly & Spent Mayfly (D)**<br>Hook Size 8<br> | Cream or white body with blue dun & badger cock wing | Dun: skip over surface<br><br>Spent: still | Surface | May<br>or<br>June |
| **Method-Tip** — When fish taking mayfly dun, dap or skip across water. Pause a few secs before striking. For spent mayfly, it should be left still in the surface film. | | | | |

| Colour | Best Retrieve | Best Depth | Best Month | Pattern Wet or dry |
|---|---|---|---|---|
| Varies<br><br>See availability chart on page 70 | 1) Still, slow or med-fast<br>2) Cast to rise – expect fast take | In or on surface<br><br>Surface film | Gen<br><br>Gen | **Midge Pupa (W) (Buzzer) See also Adult Midge**<br>Hook Size 12–16<br><br> |
| **Method-Tip** — 1) Represents pupae rising to the top to hatch. 2) Use when trout rising. | | | | |
| As prev. entry with buoyant head | Any | Surface | Gen | **Midge – Suspender Buzzer (Hatching Pupa)**<br>Hook Size 12–16<br><br> |
| **Method-Tip** — Represents midge hanging in surface film preparing to hatch – mount on greased leader stopped with blood knots every 2–3ft or fish from boat over deep water (grease and allow to drift – silence essential). | | | | |
| White red & silver body with mallard wing | Med | Any | Gen | **Missionary (W)**<br>Hook Size 6–10<br><br> |
| **Method-Tip** — Whole feather wing allows it to sink slowly which sometimes proves irresistible to trout – watch for takes on the drop. | | | | |

| Pattern<br>Wet or Dry | Colour | Best<br>Retrieve | Best<br>Depth | Best<br>Month |
|---|---|---|---|---|
| **Montana (W)**<br>Hook Size 6–8<br> | Green<br>or<br>black<br>with<br>yellow | Slow | Any | Gen |
| **Method-Tip** — Large nymph imitation: use all depths on long leader. | | | | |
| **Muddler Minnow (W)**<br>Hook Size 6 or 8<br> | Grey-<br>brown | Med to<br>slow | Just<br>under<br>or in<br>surface | Gen<br>but<br>try<br>Aug<br>Sept |
| **Method-Tip** — Especially good when trout chasing fry. Makes attractive wake. | | | | |
| **Ombudsman (W)**<br>Hook Size 8–12<br> | Green<br>with long<br>speck'd<br>brown<br>wing | Slow<br>then<br>steady<br>in later<br>season | Deep<br>early<br>then<br>surface | Apr<br>May<br>& Sept<br>Oct |
| **Method-Tip** — General pattern but good imitation of alder larva when it should be fished on sinking line and retrieved slowly along the bottom with frequent pauses. | | | | |

| Colour | Best Retrieve | Best Depth | Best Month | Pattern Wet or dry |
|--------|---------------|------------|------------|---------------------|
| White & orange | Slow near bottom but fast in surface | Any | Gen | **Persuader (W)** Hook Size 8–10 |
| **Method-Tip** — Try just under surface when trout rising here and there – watch for take as it slowly sinks. | | | | |
| Silver & red with black hackle & teal wing | Fast & jerky | Deep but surface near shore in Jul & Aug | Gen | **Peter Ross (W)** Hook Size 10–14 |
| **Method-Tip** — Imitation of small fry and freshwater shrimp – try on floating line near bank when sticklebacks and other fry leave weeds in July and August. | | | | |
| Red-brown | Sink & draw | Deep | Gen | **Pheasant Tail Nymph – Weighted (W)** Hook Size 10–16 |
| **Method-Tip** — Emulates immature nymphs of upwinged flies: mount alone on point of a long leader on floating line. *Continued overleaf* | | | | |

| Pattern<br>Wet or Dry | Colour | Best<br>Retrieve | Best<br>Depth | Best<br>Month |
|---|---|---|---|---|
| **Pheasant Tail Nymph – Not Weighted (WD)** | | Sink &<br>draw<br>or still<br>on surface | Any | Gen |
| **Method-Tip** — Try small in evenings near surface during caenis hatch. Cast to fish and leave still. | | | | |
| **Polystickle (W)**<br>Hook Size 6 or 8 | Orange<br>& poly-<br>thene | Fast | Any | Gen,<br>but best<br>in July<br>Aug<br>Sept |
| **Method-Tip** — Try when fry leave shallows for deeper water. | | | | |
| **PVC Nymph (W)**<br>Hook Size 12–17 | Olive<br>brown<br>with<br>PVC<br>cover | Sink &<br>draw | Deep | Gen |
| **Method-Tip** — Be alert for takes as it sinks. | | | | |

| Colour | Best Retrieve | Best Depth | Best Month | Pattern Wet or dry |
|--------|---------------|------------|------------|--------------------|
| Red or green with buff thorax | Very slow with tweeks | Bottom | Apr May | **Red or Green Larvae (W)** Hook Size 8–12 |
| **Method-Tip** — Emulates midge larvae. | | | | |
| Red | Slow dribble | Deep or as bob fly | Gen | **Red Palmer (W or D)** Hook Size 8–12 |
| **Method-Tip** — General pattern: fish dry in evenings but most effective dribbled through surface from early June. | | | | |
| Ginger body with red hackle | Skate or twitch | Surface | July Aug Sept | **Red Sedge (D)** Hook Size 8–10 |
| **Method-Tip** — Fish static or skate fly through surface causing wake. | | | | |

| Pattern<br>Wet or Dry | Colour | Best Retrieve | Best Depth | Best Month |
|---|---|---|---|---|
| **Red Spinner (W)**<br>Hook Size 12 or 14<br> | Dark red with gold rib & red hackle | Still | Surface | Gen |
| **Method-Tip** — Represents spent insect: cast to rising fish and leave in surface film. | | | | |
| **Sedge Pupa (W)**<br>Hook Size 10–12<br> | Cream brown orange or green | Med pace with pauses | Deep or near surface | Late June<br>July<br>Aug<br>Sept |
| **Method-Tip** — Fish in 2 ways – 1) Midwater to near bottom or 2) (During late afternoon and early evening but takes at any time) near surface on a sink or floating line. Green for Jul/Jul. Cream in Sep. | | | | |
| **Shrimper (Leaded) (W)**<br>Hook Size 10–14<br> | Olive brown with PVC back & buff hackle | Very slow pulls with pauses | On bottom in shallow water | Gen |
| **Method-Tip** — Best early when cold: try on long leader near weeds and inflows / outflows. Watch for gentle takes as it sinks. | | | | |

| Colour | Best Retrieve | Best Depth | Best Month | Pattern Wet or dry |
|---|---|---|---|---|
| Brown & silver | Slow in day – faster near surface later | Any | Gen | **Silver March Brown (W)** Hook Size 10–14 |
| **Method-Tip** — Use on bottom in shallows or near surface when evening sedge hatch. | | | | |
| Silver poly-thene & brown | Medium fast | Just below surface | May June July | **Sinfoil's Fry (D)** Hook Size 8–12 |
| **Method-Tip** — Use when trout feed on tiny fry in shallows – good cast from boat to shore. | | | | |
| Black | Leave still | Surface film | July Aug | **Snail (Floating Cork) (D)** Hook Size 10–14 |
| **Method-Tip** — When fish nose and tail as if taking caenis or small midge, cast to vicinity of rise. | | | | |

| Pattern Wet or Dry | Colour | Best Retrieve | Best Depth | Best Month |
|---|---|---|---|---|
| **Stick Fly (W)** Hook Size 8–10 | Bronze body & honey hackle | Slow | Deep on bottom | Gen |
| **Method-Tip** — Caddis grub imitation. With a green tag, useful for damsel. | | | | |
| **Stonefly (W)** Hook Size 8–10 | Brown | Slow | On bottom | Gen |
| **Method-Tip** — Natural crawls towards shore. | | | | |
| **Suspender Buzzer** | See Midge Pupa | | | |
| **Sweeny Todd (W)** Hook Size 6–14 | Magenta & black | Vary | Vary | Gen |
| **Method-Tip** — Try different sizes. | | | | |

| Colour | Best Retrieve | Best Depth | Best Month | Pattern Wet or dry |
|--------|---------------|------------|------------|--------------------|
| Black | Slow | Deep in shallow water | Apr May June | **Tadpolly (W)** Hook Size 10 or 12 |
| **Method-Tip** — Fish on its own on the point. | | | | |
| Green with light red hackle & teal wing | Med fast | Deep | Gen | **Teal & Green (W)** Hook Size 8–14 |
| **Method-Tip** — General pattern but good early. Green is one of a series of body colours. | | | | |
| Black body & wing with green tail | Vary | Any | Gen | **Viva (W)** Hook Size 6–10 |
| **Method-Tip** — Good all-round lure. Try when nothing else works. Often saves a blank day. | | | | |

| Pattern<br>Wet or Dry | Colour | Best<br>Retrieve | Best<br>Depth | Best<br>Month |
|---|---|---|---|---|
| **Walker's Sedge (D)**<br>Hook Size 8–10 | Chest-<br>nut<br>body<br>with<br>red wing<br>& hackle | Draw<br>along<br>surface<br>making<br>wake | Surface | Gen |
| **Method-Tip** — Waterproof and skate over surface lifting rod as retrieve is made. Sometimes taken in pauses between pulls. | | | | |
| **Watery Dun (D)**<br>Hook Size 12–14 | Pale<br>yellow | Still<br>or<br>tweek | Surface | Gen |
| **Method-Tip** — Cast to rising fish and leave in surface. | | | | |
| **Welsh Partridge<br>(W or D)**<br>Hook Size 12–16 | Claret<br>&<br>white<br>with<br>part-<br>ridge<br>hackle | Slow<br>with<br>pauses | Deep in<br>colder<br>months<br>& near<br>top in<br>summer | Gen |
| **Method-Tip** — General pattern: try small and dry when no fish being caught. | | | | |

| Colour | Best Retrieve | Best Depth | Best Month | Pattern Wet or dry |
|--------|---------------|------------|------------|--------------------|
| Orange & silver | Any | Any | Gen | **Whisky Fly (W)** Hook Size 6–10  |
| **Method-Tip** — Lure: particularly good in latter half of season; reputed to be attractive to big fish. | | | | |
| Gold & red with quill wing | Varied | Any | Gen | **Wickham's Fancy (WD)** Hook Size 12–16  |
| **Method-Tip** — Normally wet but effective small and dry for smutting fish. | | | | |
| Bronze & black | Slow | On or near bottom or semi-dry in surface | Gen | **Worm Fly (W)** Hook Size 10–12 |
| **Method-Tip** — Resembles several species: try deep when nothing moving. | | | | |

| Pattern<br>Wet or Dry | Colour | Best<br>Retrieve | Best<br>Depth | Best<br>Month |
|---|---|---|---|---|
| **Yellow Humpy (D)**<br>Hook Size 10–12<br> | Deer hair with yellow belly | Still or tweek | Surface | Gen |
| | **Method-Tip** — This bushy fly might be called a lure. Often takes if left static. | | | |

# Notes on own flies

| Colour | Best Retrieve | Best Depth | Best Month | Pattern Wet or dry |
|--------|---------------|------------|------------|--------------------|
|        |               |            |            |                    |
| Method-Tip — |         |            |            |                    |
|        |               |            |            |                    |
| Method-Tip — |         |            |            |                    |

| Pattern Wet or Dry | Colour | Best Retrieve | Best Depth | Best Month |
|---|---|---|---|---|
| | | | | |
| | **Method-Tip —** | | | |
| | | | | |
| | **Method-Tip —** | | | |
| | | | | |
| | **Method-Tip —** | | | |

| Colour | Best Retrieve | Best Depth | Best Month | Pattern Wet or dry |
|---|---|---|---|---|
| | | | | |
| Method-Tip — | | | | |
| | | | | |
| Method-Tip — | | | | |
| | | | | |
| Method-Tip — | | | | |

# Monthly guide to fly selection

These pages are designed to help the angler select an appropriate imitation, cast or lure for the time of year, but, while fish and their food do their best, the following information is packaged for our understanding and it will be of more use if this is remembered.

If spring is unusually cold and summer late in coming, then it is up to the angler to make adjustments. Take into account the prevailing weather and other considerations, like:

- *Depth*. Trout are cold-blooded and their body temperatures are roughly the same as that of the water – when it is cold, the fish are slow and lazy, so a gentle retrieve might be more successful. Whether particularly hot or cold, the majority of the stock will probably be deep where it is either warmer or cooler.
- *Line*. In cold weather and because banks of most stillwaters slope gradually and a normal cast will cover most depths, a slow sinking line is best – fast sinkers need to be retrieved fairly quickly to avoid snagging obstructions on the lake bed and are better used in deep water from a boat. In almost all other conditions a floating line is usually best.

Try to identify the food the trout may be interested in by observation and use of the Insect Identification Table or, if you are successful, by analysing the stomach contents of the fish.

Because of our unreliable climate, the months in this guide are combined as considered suitable but, depending on the prevailing conditions or to gain an overall picture, please read the months before and/or after.


# March and early April

Unless the weather is unusually warm, boat fishing early in the season is a waste of time. If it is preferred for some other reason, remember – as on the bank – if you have no luck, keep moving. At this time fish are generally on the bottom, but most of their food is in water between five and fifteen feet deep, so slow moving trout form small shoals in relatively restricted areas. Flies should be retrieved very slowly, inched back patiently, and you will just have to keep moving until you find the fish.

In March and April freshwater Shrimp are often present in shallow water (Shrimper), Alder Larva leave their burrows and creep towards the shore. Caddis, Damsel Fly Nymphs and Red or Green Larva of chironomids squirm on the lake bed and, as it warms up, some of the latter may start to hatch early in the evenings (Midge Pupa, Hatching Midge Pupa, Adult Buzzer, Blae and Black). On windy days, look out for Hawthorn Flies blown onto the water.

*Best colours*

In March and April darker colours are more successful. If imitative patterns fail, try a black or white marabou lure.

## Imitative patterns

Alder Larva
Black and Peacock
Black Pennel
Black Zulu
Blae and Black
Butcher
Caddis Fly
Damsel Nymph

Hawthorn Fly
Mallard and Claret
Pheasant Tail Nymph
Red/Green Larvae
Shrimper
Silver March Brown
Stick Fly
Tadpolly

## Lures

Ace of Spades
Appetizer
Baby Doll
Black Chenille
Dog Nobbler (black or white)
Worm Fly

Jersey Herd
Missionary
Ombudsman
Viva

## Casts* (mix and match)

| Point | Dropper | Bob |
|---|---|---|
| Alder Larva | Midge Pupa | Suspender Buzzer |
| Stick Fly | Blae and Black | Butcher |
| Black Midge | Black and Peacock | Midge Pupa |
| Viva | Zulu | Mallard and Claret |
| Appetizer | | Black Pennel |
| Caddis | | Soldier Palmer |
| Worm Fly | | |

* 18–24ft leader with flies 3ft apart.

# Late April and May

If spring is on time there is good sport for the angler. In late April most trout will still be feeding deeply and the bank is still best unless the water is clear and the light is bright, when very deep water may be fished from a boat using large black lures. As the weeks go by and the weather begins to settle, the water temperature climbs. Rises may then be expected with the trout feeding on Midge Pupa.

Insect life carries on in much the same vein with Caddis, Damsel Fly Nymphs and the Red or Green Larva. Midge Pupae are the exception with increased numbers causing some of the best rises of the season. From mid-May expect activity early in the mornings and late in the afternoons as the trout feed heavily on Black or Grey Midge Pupae, then, towards the end of the month, smaller Olive-green Pupae. Establish whether the fish are chasing emerging pupae to the surface or taking them as they hang in the surface film (see 'Rise Forms'). Often, at the end of May, Lake Olives may be observed hatching and drifting on the surface, and in the shallows Tadpoles are often active.

*Best colours*

Black or white are still the best colours until mid-May when nymphs and flies adopt lighter tints – olive greens and mottled browns with gold – but black is still good particularly when there are Hawthorns etc. on the water.

Towards the end of May try lures of warmer colours such as orange and yellow.

*Imitative patterns*

Adult Midge
Alder Larva
Black and Peacock
Black Pennel
Black Zulu
Blae and Black
Butcher
Caddis Fly
Damsel Nymph
Hawthorn Fly

Lake Olive
Mallard and Claret
Midge (vary colours)
Pheasant Tail Nymph
Red/Green Larvae
Shrimper
Silver March Brown
Stick Fly
Tadpolly

*Lures*

Ace of Spades
Appetizer
Baby Doll
Black Chenille
Black Ghost
Dog Nobbler (black, orange, yellow, white)
Worm Fly

Jersey Herd
Missionary
Ombudsman
Viva
Whisky Fly

*Casts\* (mix and match)*

| *Point* | *Dropper* | *Bob* |
| --- | --- | --- |
| Stick Fly | Midge Pupa | Suspender Buzzer |

| | | |
|---|---|---|
| Black Buzzer | (black, orange | Soldier Palmer |
| Hawthorn | or green) | Wickham's Fancy |
| Viva | | Gold-ribbed |
| | | Hare's Ear |
| Appetizer | Greenwell's | Red Palmer |
| Red Palmer | Glory (wet) | Blae and Black |
| Midge Pupa | | Red Palmer |

In the first 2 weeks of May, try a trio of adult midge in the surface film. If trout rise to the pupae (try different colours) but will not take them, try a Gold-ribbed Hare's Ear on the point and retrieve figure of 8, experimenting with the speed.

If trout appear to be rising to floating duns then mount a single size 12 dry Greenwell's Glory and cast to individual rise.

## June/July

Early June follows on in much the same way as May with midge as the trout's main diet but as temperatures increase rises take place in the cooler early mornings and evenings. Swirling daytime rises to various up-winged flies are common, especially between eleven and three o'clock (see Dun Identification Table page 89). The early and late feeding pattern is well established by the end of the month and continues through July when daytime rises become rarer.

In July it is best to get to the lake around dawn, but as

the month passes the midge hatches diminish slightly and the best rises are usually in the late afternoon. Remember, in hot temperatures the bulk of the stock will be in cooler deeper water (see *Bright, calm conditions* or *Hot, calm summer days* pages 92–93). On hot, still days fishing can be frustrating and expect a Caenis hatch. The trout may also take Daphnia, a tiny crustacean member of the plankton family which they drink in like soup, at levels dependent on the light – early mornings Daphnia are high in the water and deepest when sun is strongest (try a bright fluorescent green or orange lure).

New additions to the trout menu are the Caenis and Daphnia, Sedge, various Up-winged Flies, Tadpoles in the shallows and adult Damsel Nymphs, which they chase just under the surface as they swim to the shore. Towards the end of July some fish will begin chasing Fry. Watch for Flying Ants and Snails.

*Best colours*

In early June, black and white lures are still favourites but try hotter colours – red, orange, yellow – in the latter half. For artificial flies and nymphs, try olive early then gingers, and reds. Continue with the white and brighter lures into July but also try orange and gold, and lime green. Similarly, start July with ginger and red flies and nymphs but try buff towards the end of the month.

## Imitative patterns

Adult Midge
Caddis
G and H Sedge
Greenwell's Glory
Invicta
Midge Pupa
Polystickle
Red Sedge
Silver March Brown
Tadpolly
Wickham's Fancy
Black and Peacock

Lake Olive
Damsel Nymph
Gold-ribbed Hare's Ear
Grey Duster
Mallard and Claret
Suspender Buzzer
Red Palmer
Sedge Pupae
Sinfoil's Fry
Walker's Sedge
Last Hope

## Lures

Aylott's Orange
Black Bear's Hair
Coachman
Montana
Whisky Fly
Yellow Humpy

Baby Doll
Cat's Whisker
Dog Nobbler
Viva
Worm Fly

## Casts (mix and match)

| Point | Dropper | Bob |
|---|---|---|
| *Midge Pupa | Midge Pupa | Midge Pupa |
| Dry Sedge | Collyer's | Red Palmer |
| Damsel | Green | Suspender Buzzer |

| | | |
|---|---|---|
| Stick Fly | Teal and Blue | Soldier Palmer |
| Sinfoil's Fry | | Wickham's Fancy |
| Viva | Greenwell's | Grenadier |
| Invicta | Glory (wet) | Butcher |
| Appetizer | | |
| Whisky Fly | Gold-ribbed | |
| | Hare's Ear | |

*Use various colours. Try to match what is available.

## August

Like the last two weeks of July, fishing in August can be difficult and catches poor. There are reasons apart from the heat: there are fewer fish and those who have escaped have learnt prudence. These wary fish are usually in excellent condition but following the plentiful provisions of early summer they feed less enthusiastically.

Expect a Caenis hatch. Watch out for trout taking Daphnia (try a bright fluorescent green or orange lure). Also, like July, rises to Midge are more likely in the early mornings and evenings, yet Fry and Damsel Nymphs may be taken at any time. While Cream or Orange Sedge Pupa are sometimes popular from early afternoon, most of the time the trout lie doggo in the cooler deeper water (see *Bright, calm conditions* or *Hot, calm summer days* pages 92-93). In late August, when the days shorten and the temperature falls, the fishing improves as they feed on Fry and last Damsel and sometimes Snails in the surface, and

Corixa in the shallows. Daddy Long Legs are added to the menu. Also, Lake Olives reappear and often, Flying Ants.

*Best colours*

Lures: orange, red, gold, pink.
Flies and Nymphs: red, ginger, pale greens, beige, buff, pinky grey.

*Imitative Patterns*

| | |
|---|---|
| Adult Midge | Lake Olive |
| Amber Nymph | Butcher |
| Caddis | Daddy Long Legs |
| Damsel Nymph | Corixa |
| G and H Sedge | Gold-ribbed Hare's Ear |
| Greenwell's Glory | Grey Duster |
| Invicta | Mallard and Claret |
| Midge Pupa | Suspender Buzzer |
| Polystickle | Red Palmer |
| Red Sedge | Sedge Pupae |
| Silver March Brown | Sinfoil's Fry |
| Tadpolly | Walker's Sedge |
| Wickham's Fancy | Last Hope |
| Dunkeld | |

*Lures*

| | |
|---|---|
| Aylott's Orange | Baby Doll (Try pink) |
| Black Bear's Hair | Cat's Whisker |

Coachman
Montana
Whisky Fly
Black and Orange Marabou
Muddler

Dog Nobbler
Viva
Worm Fly

*Casts (Mix and Match)*

| *Point* | *Dropper* | *Bob* |
|---|---|---|
| *Midge Pupa | Midge Pupa | Midge Pupa |
| Stick Fly | Teal and Green | Soldier Palmer |
| Sinfoil's Fry | Invicta | Wickham's Fancy |
| Viva | Greenwell's Glory | Grenadier |
| Corixa | (wet) | Suspender Buzzer |
| Appetizer | | |
| Whisky Fly | | |
| Damsel Nymph | | |

*Use various colours. Try to match the natural.

# September/October

Success in autumn is dependent on the weather. If conditions are settled, September can be excellent from dawn to dusk with trout feeding on or near the surface all day, and if October continues in the same way then so do the fish, although their activity does tend to tail off. Larger fish, including brown trout driven by spawning instincts, feed in shallow areas. If the weather is poor, the water temperature drops quickly and evening rises decrease as insect life wanes, and it is no longer necessary to get to the bank early. The trout seem more aggressive in their search for food and the techniques and artificials of the early season are useful once again. Sinking lines fished deeply with strong (6lb) leaders retrieved slowly cheat strong winds.

September continues as August but it is the month when Daddy Long Legs are seen in large numbers, and Lake Olives may appear in the early afternoon. Although Midge hatches continue, the insects are smaller and darker, numbers decrease and hatches may be spread throughout the day. Often the fish will feed on Corixidae or chase Sedge Pupae or adult Sedge skating on the surface and Fry near the bank – it is also the time when Fry leave the shallows so it is worth trying patterns in deeper water.

*Best colours*

Lures: As August (orange, red, gold, pink) at first, but as

September progresses, black is useful again. In October, black or white.

Flies and Nymphs: red, ginger, pale greens, beige, buff turning darker later in September; then even drabber for October.

## Imitative patterns

| | |
|---|---|
| Adult Midge | Lake Olive |
| Amber Nymph | Butcher |
| Caddis | Daddy Long Legs |
| Damsel Nymph | Corixa |
| G and H Sedge | Gold-ribbed Hare's Ear |
| Greenwell's Glory | Dunkeld |
| Invicta | Mallard and Claret |
| Midge Pupa | Suspender Buzzer |
| Polystickle | Red Palmer |
| Red Sedge | Sedge Pupae |
| Silver March Brown | Sinfoil's Fry |
| Tadpolly | Walker's Sedge |
| Wickham's Fancy | Stick Fly |

## Lures

| | |
|---|---|
| Ace of Spades | Sweeny Todd |
| Aylott's Orange | Baby Doll |
| Black Bear's Hair | Cat's Whisker |
| Coachman | Dog Nobbler |
| Montana | Viva |

Whisky Fly
Black and Orange Marabou
Missionary

Worm Fly
Muddler
Jack Frost

*Casts (mix and match)*

| *Point* | *Dropper* | *Bob* |
|---|---|---|
| Midge Pupa | Midge Pupa | Midge Pupa |
| Stick Fly | Teal and Green | Soldier Palmer |
| Sinfoil's Fry | Invicta | Wickham's Fancy |
| Viva | Grenadier | |
| Corixa | | Suspender |
| Buzzer | | |
| Appetizer | | |
| Whisky Fly | Greenwell's | |
| | Glory (wet) | |
| Jack Frost | | |
| Missionary | | |
| Muddler | | |

# At-a-glance availability table

| Insect | Apr | May | June | July | Aug | Sept | Oct |
|---|---|---|---|---|---|---|---|
| Alder Larvae | ■ | ■ | ■ | | | | |
| Beetles | | ■ | ■ | ■ | ■ | ■ | |
| Corixidae | ■ | ■ | ■ | ■ | ■ | ■ | ■ |
| Daddy Long Legs | | | | ■ | ■ | ■ | |
| Damsel Nymphs | ■ | ■ | ■ | ■ | ■ | | |
| Fry | | | | | ■ | ■ | ■ |
| Mayflies | | ■ | | | | | |
| Midge Black | ■ | ■ | | ■ | ■ | ■ | |
| Brown | | | ■ | ■ | ■ | ■ | ■ |
| Green(S) | ■ | ■ | ■ | ■ | ■ | ■ | ■ |
| Green (L) | | | | ■ | | | |
| Orange | ■ | ■ | | | | | |
| Red | | | | ■ | ■ | ■ | |
| Sedges | | | ■ | ■ | ■ | ■ | ■ |
| Snails | | | | ■ | ■ | ■ | |
| Stoneflies | ■ | ■ | ■ | ■ | ■ | ■ | ■ |
| Up-winged Flies Claret Duns | | ■ | ■ | ■ | | | |
| Lake Olives | | ■ | ■ | | | ■ | |
| Pond Olives | ■ | ■ | ■ | ■ | ■ | ■ | ■ |
| Sepia Duns | ■ | ■ | | | | | |
| Blue winged Olives | | | | ■ | ■ | ■ | ■ |

# Insect identification and behaviour

This chapter contains information on some of the more common British insects to be found on the trout's menu. Each entry shows a brief description to help the angler identify any insect etc. he may observe – because of the difficulty of distinguishing between up-winged flies, there is a table on page 89 to help.

The table also details the insects' lifecycles, any special movements, or depths and habitats, knowledge of which might prove helpful to the angler in locating the trout's feeding places and presenting an artificial.

On the right of these details there are suggestions for which artificial to try.

| Insect/Length | Month | Colours | Wing No. | Wing Colours | Tail No. |
|---|---|---|---|---|---|
| **Alder Larva**<br><br>c 25mm | Mar<br>Apr<br>May<br>to<br>June | Buff head & thorax with tapered brown abdomen | – | – | – |

| **Movement/Depth** | **Flies** |
|---|---|
| Crawls on bottom towards shore to pupate and hatch (adult rarely of use because it does not fall onto water in any great numbers). | Alder Larva<br>Ombudsman |

| Insect/Length | Month | Colours | Wing No. | Wing Colours | Tail No. |
|---|---|---|---|---|---|
| **Beetle**<br><br>Various | June<br>July<br>Aug | Black | – | – | – |

| **Movement/Depth** | **Flies** |
|---|---|
| Terrestrial beetles blown onto water. | Black and Peacock<br>Try to match with what you have. |

| Insect/Length | Month | Colours | Wing No. | Wing Colours | Tail No. |
|---|---|---|---|---|---|
| **Blue Winged Olive**<br><br>**Nymph**<br><br>c 12mm | July<br>Aug<br>Sept | Brown thorax with darker brown wing cases and mottled brown abdomen | – | – | 3 |

| **Movement/Depth**<br>Usually found in streams and only occasionally in lakes.<br><br>Found in weeds and likes 7 to 10ft of water. | **Flies**<br>Gold Ribbed Hare's Ear<br><br>Pheasant Tail |
|---|---|

| Insect/Length | Month | Colours | Wing No. | Wing Colours | Tail No. |
|---|---|---|---|---|---|
| **Blue Winged Olive**<br><br>**Dun**<br><br>c 12mm | July<br>Aug<br>Sept | Olive | 4 | Dark blue – grey | 3 |

| **Movement/Depth**<br>Usually found in streams and only occasionally seen on lakes.<br><br>Hatches on surface where it dries for a few minutes giving the angler good opportunity for dry fly fishing. | **Flies**<br>Pheasant Tail (dry)<br><br>Gold Ribbed Hare's Ear |
|---|---|

**Caddis** – see Sedge Larvae

| Insect/Length | Month | Colours | Wing No. | Wing Colours | Tail No. |
|---|---|---|---|---|---|
| **Caenis Nymph**<br><br>c 6mm | May<br>June<br>July<br>Aug | Dark thorax with brown abdomen | – | – | 3 |

| Movement/Depth | Flies |
|---|---|
| Crawls on bottom then, from June to August, rises to surface to hatch in late afternoon/evening. Fishing difficult because of size and number. | |
| (1) Try very small Pheasant Tail Nymph or Gold Ribbed Hare's Ear. | Pheasant Tail or Gold Ribbed Hare's Ear |
| (2) Fish Black lure in surface. | Nobbler or Chenille |
| (3) Cast and leave a large dry fly. | Yellow Humpy |
| (4) Violently rip a buoyant worm fly on a well greased leader in front of moving fish, leaving a stream of bubbles. Let it return to surface and repeat. | Worm Fly |
| (5) Cast a weighted Green Nymph at fish and let it sink about 3ft (watch for take) then lift rod raising fly to surface. | Collyer's Green |
| (6) Steadily draw a Coachman just below the surface. | Coachman |

| Insect/Length | Month | Colours | Wing No. | Wing Colours | Tail No. |
|---|---|---|---|---|---|
| **Caenis Dun & Spinner** 4–6mm | June July Aug | Dark thorax with yellow, grey or cream-coloured abdomen | 2 | Pale grey to off-white | 3 |
| **Movement/Depth** Duns and Spinners very similar. Duns hatch quickly and rarely seen trapped in surface film. Fishing difficult: see Caenis Nymph on previous page. | | | | **Flies** Last Hope or Grey Duster | |
| **Claret Nymph** c 13mm | May June July | Dark reddish brown | – | – | 3 |
| **Movement/Depth** Crawls among weed and litter of lake bed in shallower water. Poor swimmer and a build up of gas aids its rise directly to the surface. | | | | **Flies** Pheasant Tail Gold Ribbed Hare's Ear | |
| **Claret Dun** 6–8mm | May June July | Brown | 4 | Dark grey | 3 |
| **Movement/Depth** Hatching usually between midday and early afternoon, the emerged adults sit on the surface drying wings for some time. | | | | **Flies** Autumn Dun | |

| Insect/Length | Month | Colours | Wing No. | Wing Colours | Tail No. |
|---|---|---|---|---|---|
| **Claret Spinner**<br><br>6–8mm | May<br>June<br>July | Dark shiny brown with red tinge on tail. Abdomen ringed with lighter joints | 4 | Translucent with pale brown veins | 3 |
| **Movement/Depth**<br>From early evening spent insects fall into surface film. | | | | **Flies**<br>Red Spinner | |
| **Corixid (Adult)**<br><br>c 14mm | Gen | Varied | 2 | Wing cases vary from yellow to olive to dark brown | – |
| **Movement/Depth**<br>Beetle-like adults take to the air in mid to late summer. | | | | **Flies**<br>Larger Corixa | |
| **Corixid (Water Boatmen) Nymph**<br>c 14mm | Gen but July – Sept best | Pale cream | – | Translucent wing cases | – |
| **Movement/Depth**<br>Likes weed in shallow water but they regularly collect air from surface, swimming with rapid jerky zig-zag movements, descending slower with trapped air bubble. | | | | **Flies**<br>The Corixa or Corixa Plastazote | |

| Insect/Length | Month | Colours | Wing No. | Wing Colours | Tail No. |
|---|---|---|---|---|---|
| **Daddy Long Legs (Crane Fly)** c 20mm | July Aug Sept | Grey brown or ochre | 2 | Translucent | – |

| **Movement/Depth** | **Flies** |
|---|---|
| These terrestrial flies are often blown onto water where they lie with legs spread out behind them. | Daddy Long Legs (Crane Fly) |

| Insect/Length | Month | Colours | Wing No. | Wing Colours | Tail No. |
|---|---|---|---|---|---|
| **Damselfly Nymph** 15–35mm | Mar Apr May June July Aug | Green but shortly before hatching brown case forms over thorax | – | – | 3 |

| **Movement/Depth** | **Flies** |
|---|---|
| Young nymph clings to weed where it blends in. Prefers to crawl rather than swim. As season progresses the trout take them more freely until mid-August when adults finish hatching. To hatch they either climb up or swim from weed to shore. | Damsel Nymph or Damsel Wiggle Nymph |

| **Daphnia** | Trout often drink in this tiny crustacean member of the plankton family like soup at a depth dependent on light. In the early mornings Daphnia drifts high in the water. At noon, when the sun is strongest, it is at its deepest. Try a bright fluorescent green or orange lure. |
|---|---|

| Insect/Length | Month | Colours | Wing No. | Wing Colours | Tail No. |
|---|---|---|---|---|---|
| **Flying Ant**<br>6–10mm | July<br>Aug | Black or dark red with white wings | – | – | – |

| **Movement/Depth** | **Flies** |
|---|---|
| These terrestrial ants seem to all fly on the same day. Trout often go mad for them when blown onto water. | Blae and Black<br>Try to match from fly box |

| Insect/Length | Month | Colours |
|---|---|---|
| **Fry**<br><br>Various | July<br>Aug<br>Sept | Various: sticklebacks, minnow and coarse fry are spawned in spring. By Aug/Sep the fry, who shoal around weeds in shallows, are up to 2in long. |

| **Movement/Depth** | **Flies** |
|---|---|
| They feed on nymphs, larvae etc. in shallow weed beds or near vertical surfaces of jetties etc.<br><br>When attacked by trout charging their shoal, the fry flee with a darting action, sometimes with pauses. | Polystickle<br><br><br>Cat's Whisker<br>Appetizer<br>Church Fry<br>Jack Frost<br><br>Sinfoil's Fry<br>White or Orange Nobbler |

| Insect/Length | Month | Colours | Wing No. | Wing Colours | Tail No. |
|---|---|---|---|---|---|
| **Hawthorn Fly** | April May | Black (with trailing legs) | 2 | Grey-white | – |
| **Movement/Depth** This terrestrial fly is often blown onto water. On a windy day they can be present in great numbers. | | | | **Flies** Hawthorn Fly Black and Peacock | |
| **Lake Olive Nymph** c 13mm | Mainly May June & Aug Sept | Black thorax with mottled yellow brown abdomen | – | – | 3 |
| **Movement/Depth** Likes weed in bays and inlets and 5–15ft of water. Swims fast for short distances. Often taken as it floats to surface to hatch. | | | | **Flies** Greenwell's Glory (W) Lake Olive Gold Ribbed Hare's Ear | |

| Insect/Length | Month | Colours | Wing No. | Wing Colours | Tail No. |
|---|---|---|---|---|---|
| **Lake Olive Dun**<br><br>c 12mm | May<br>June<br>&<br>Aug<br>Sept | May Jun = dark grey-green thorax & olive abdomen.<br>Aug Sep = rusty olive thorax | – | Grey early ginger later | 2 |

| Movement/Depth | Flies |
|---|---|
| Early summer duns are larger and darker. | Greenwell's Glory<br>Lake Olive<br>Gold Ribbed<br>Hare's Ear |

| Insect/Length | Month | Colours | Wing No. | Wing Colours | Tail No. |
|---|---|---|---|---|---|
| **Lake Olive Spinner**<br><br>c 12mm | May<br>June<br>&<br>Aug<br>Sept | Thorax = dark brown.<br>Abdomen = rust on top & grey-green beneath | 2 | Glossy translucent with brown tinge | 2 |

| Movement/Depth | Flies |
|---|---|
| After laying eggs spent fly lies on surface. | Greenwell's Glory<br>Lake Olive |

| Insect/Length | Month | Colours | Wing No. | Wing Colours | Tail No. |
|---|---|---|---|---|---|
| **Mayfly Nymph**<br><br>c 25mm | May<br>June | Pale fawn with dull brown thorax | – | – | 3 |

| **Movement/Depth** | **Flies** |
|---|---|
| Crawls and burrows in lake bed but leaves shelter a week or so before rising directly and quickly to surface to hatch. | Mayfly Nymph (Walker's) |

| Insect/Length | Month | Colours | Wing No. | Wing Colours | Tail No. |
|---|---|---|---|---|---|
| **Mayfly Dun & Spinner**<br><br>c 20mm | May<br>June | Dun = dark brown head & thorax and creamy grey abdomen with brown or grey top.<br>Spinner = brighter creamy white body with brown rings on last 3 segments | 4 | Dun: dull yellow-grey with heavy brown veining<br><br><br>Spinner: bright transparent with rust colour veins | 3 |

| **Movement/Depth** | **Flies** |
|---|---|
| Hatches usually occur between the 3rd week in May and the 1st week in June. Trout often reticent about taking hatching dun unless prolific then they will go mad for them.<br>Spent Mayflies lie in surface film. | Mayfly<br><br><br>Spent Mayfly |

| Insect/Length | Month | Colours | Wing No. | Wing Colours | Tail No. |
|---|---|---|---|---|---|
| **Midge Larva**<br><br>c 20mm | Gen | Several species ranging from translucent to ochre to brown but green and red most common. | | | |
| **Movement/Depth**<br>Worm-like larva propels itself with figure of eight motion on or near bottom. | | | | **Flies**<br>Red or Green Larvae or Blood worm | |
| **Midge Pupa**<br><br>c 13mm | Gen | Ranges from grey, ochre, brown, green, red to black with dark head & thorax. Tufts of white gills protrude from thorax and they have similar short tails *(see Insect Availability Table on page 70 for colours). | | | |
| **Movement/Depth**<br>Pupal stage lasts only days. They hover close to bottom then rise slowly to surface where they swim just below or hang motionless in the film which, on calm still days, they have difficulty breaking. | | | | **Flies**<br>(Hatching)<br>Midge Pupa<br>Footballer | |

| Insect/Length | Month | Colours | Wing No. | Wing Colours | Tail No. |
|---|---|---|---|---|---|
| **Midge Adult (Buzzer)** c 13mm | Gen | Varied with dark head & thorax | 2 | Translucent | – |
| **Movement/Depth** Hatch takes only seconds then adult off to bank to mate. Females return to release their eggs. | | | | **Flies** Adult Buzzer | |
| **Pond Olive Nymph** c 12mm | Gen | Brown thorax with darker brown wing cases and mottled ochre and brown abdomen often with olive tinge. | | | 3 |
| **Movement/Depth** Rapid swimmers with undulating movement found in weed or in litter on lake bed. Swims to surface to hatch (usually around midday). | | | | **Flies** Gold Ribbed Hare's Ear | |
| **Pond Olive Dun** c 12mm | Gen | Dark olive thorax with olive grey abdomen usually with orange tinge at rear | 2 | Dark blue grey | 2 |
| **Movement/Depth** After hatching it leaves water almost immediately therefore trout tend to concentrate on the hatching nymphs. | | | | **Flies** Greenwell's Glory | |

| Insect/Length | Month | Colours | Wing No. | Wing Colours | Tail No. |
|---|---|---|---|---|---|
| **Pond Olive Spinner (Apricot Spinner)** c 12mm | Gen | Olive thorax with bright apricot abdomen marked with amber | 2 | Translucent with orange at leading edge | 2 |

| **Movement/Depth** Female spinners rarely return to water before dusk but often arrive in large numbers. After laying eggs they lie dead in the surface film. | **Flies** Watery Dun |
|---|---|

| Insect/Length | Month | Colours | | |
|---|---|---|---|---|
| **Sedge Larva or Caddis** 6–24mm | May to Oct | Tapered body with dark head. This creature builds a protective case from its surroundings, e.g. weed, sand, dirt, twigs etc. Legs extend from front of body. | | |

| **Movement/Depth** Bottom dwellers which eventually emerge from their larval cases as pupae. | **Flies** Caddis Fly |
|---|---|

| Insect/Length | Month | Colours | | |
|---|---|---|---|---|
| **Sedge Pupa** 8–24mm | June to Oct | Varies from fawn to yellow to orange, green or brown | | |

| **Movement/Depth** Rise to surface to hatch. | **Flies** Sedge Pupae or for hatching sedge try Invicta |
|---|---|

| Insect/Length | Month | Colours | Wing No. | Wing Colours | Tail No. |
|---|---|---|---|---|---|
| **Sedge Fly**<br><br>8–24mm | June<br>July<br>Aug<br>Sept<br>Oct | Varied in shades from cream to red to brown to grey | 4 | – | – |
| **Movement/Depth**<br>On hatching, the large antennaed flies sometimes skitter across the surface, a disturbance which seems to attract trout, before fluttering off with abdomen down. | | | | **Flies**<br>G & H Sedge or Walker's Sedge | |
| **Sepia Nymph**<br><br>c 12mm | Apr<br>May<br>June | Dark brown | – | – | 3 |
| **Movement/Depth**<br>Poor swimmer. Crawls on bottom in deeper water then crawls into vegetation in shallows before hatching. Gas build up aids rise to surface. | | | | **Flies**<br>Sm. Brown Nymph<br>Gold Ribbed<br>Hare's Ear | |
| **Sepia Dun**<br><br>c 12mm | Apr<br>May<br>June | Dark sepia brown on top; lighter beneath | 4 | Pale fawn | 3 |
| **Movement/Depth**<br>Hatches usually around midday to early afternoon. | | | | **Flies**<br>Dry Pheasant Tail | |

| Insect/Length | Month | Colours | Wing No. | Wing Colours | Tail No. |
|---|---|---|---|---|---|
| **Sepia Spinner**<br><br>c 12mm | Apr<br>May<br>June | Dark sepia brown on top; lighter beneath | 4 | Transparent with light brown veins & grey streak on lead edges | 3 |

| **Movement/Depth** | **Flies** |
|---|---|
| Rarely on water in great numbers. | Dry Pheasant Tail |

| Insect/Length | Month | Colours | Wing Colours | Tail No. |
|---|---|---|---|---|
| **Shrimp (freshwater)**<br><br>6–24mm | Gen | Pale watery ochre back that darkens in mid-summer | Mass of legs from under body | – |

| **Movement/Depth** | **Flies** |
|---|---|
| Smooth not jerky swimmers in weed beds near inlets and outlets. | Shrimper |

| Insect/Length | Month | Colours | Wing No. | Wing Colours | Tail No. |
|---|---|---|---|---|---|
| **Stonefly Nymph**<br><br>12–25mm | Gen | Brown | – | – | 2 |

| **Movement/Depth** | **Flies** |
|---|---|
| Lives among rocks on lake bed: crawls to dry land to hatch into adult. | Stonefly |

| Insect/Length | Month | Colours | Wing No. | Wing Colours | Tail No. |
|---|---|---|---|---|---|
| **Water Beetle Larva**<br><br>6–30mm | May<br>Jun<br>Jul<br>Aug<br>Sep | Segmented pear-shaped bodies range from olive grey to brown | | | |

| **Movement/Depth**<br>Crawl on weeds and stones on bottom. | **Flies**<br>These vary and the angler must do his best from what he has available |
|---|---|

# Duns and Spinners

## Life cycle

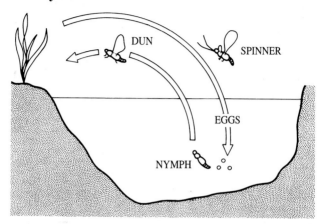

## Spinners

With the possible exception of the Pond Olive's 'apricot', the various spinners' colours are darker, yet their general appearances are more pronounced and even seem brighter: their wings are more translucent and thoraces and abdomens are glossier. The 'apricot' spinner is more decorative than her previous dun incarnation or the grey male; her legs and tails are pale green, her thorax is olive green and her abdomen is apricot yellow with orange marks which are repeated on the leading edges of glass-like wings. Other than this example the chart opposite can be used for spinners too.

# Dun Identification Table

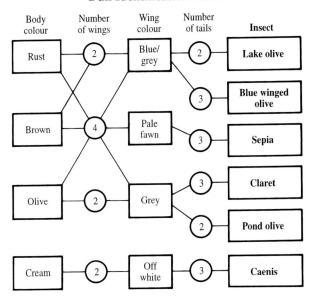

| Body colour | Number of wings | Wing colour | Number of tails | Insect |
|---|---|---|---|---|
| Rust | 2 | Blue/grey | 2 | **Lake olive** |
| | | | 3 | **Blue winged olive** |
| Brown | 4 | Pale fawn | 3 | **Sepia** |
| | | | 3 | **Claret** |
| Olive | 2 | Grey | 2 | **Pond olive** |
| Cream | 2 | Off white | 3 | **Caenis** |

(see previous page for advice about spinners)

# Unusual conditions

## Weather conditions

The cold-blooded trout's body temperature is relatively affected by that of the water, so when it is cold a fish will be lethargic. On such occasions it will stay in deep water where it is slightly warmer. Similarly, when the weather is hot and the water warms up, the fish will shelter in the now cooler deeper water. The depth presents problems but not as many as the trout's lethargy. There are also conditions other than prolonged periods of cold or hot weather to worry the angler: strong gusty winds and torrential rain can easily spoil a day's fishing. The following tips should help. Some were offered freely on the bank and proved to be successful, some are the result of experience and others, study. Some are straightforward and their reasons obvious, but there are a few odd ones. Make of them what you will, but there is little doubt many work, perhaps only because they provoke a different approach when all the usual have failed. Good luck.

## Wind

Because currents are formed by steady winds, changeable gusts over a time contrive to confuse the water and the angler. If only because of the difficulty of casting it is probably better to fish from a boat.

- Try to retrieve across any wind and current.
- Fish wind lanes formed by the convergence of two currents. Surface food is concentrated in the smoother

water of the lanes and trout like to feed upwind of them.

- Deep currents usually run in the opposite direction to the prevailing wind – fish across or upstream.

- Always try to fish on or adjacent to a lee shore: trout gather there because the water temperature is warmer and/or because any available surface food will be blown there.

- If the wind is behind you, cast to a point where the water increases in depth. The fish will gather there next to the warmer water, eating any hatching midge etc. blown out of the shallows.

- On the bank, try to choose water protected by trees or a high bank where the water is calmer. Hatching flies find it difficult to break through the surface tension of calm water. Always cast your fly to the edge of the ripple.

- Watch for land insects blown onto the water, e.g. hawthorn flies in May or daddy long legs in September.

- If the wind whips up muddy waters round the shore line, fish the edge where the water clears.

## Bad light

- Red, green and white fluorescent wool, made active by ultraviolet light that varies according to the weather and time of day, is more successful on a dull day. Yellow and orange are better on sunny days. On grey, blustery days, try a Cat's Whiskers or a Baby Doll.

# Bright, calm conditions

*Early and late in season*

- Do not thrash water.
- In clear water, try a thinly-dressed dry fly on a light line. Cast to the edge of any ripple and wait.
- Try a fry imitation and vary the depth.
- Try a buoyant nymph on a sinking line with a short leader. Let it remain still for a minute then retrieve with a slow figure of eight. Watch for crashing takes.
- Try a team of corixa. Allow them to sink then pull steadily to the surface as if they are coming up for air. Try parallel and close to the bank.
- Try a Worm Fly fished deeply.

*Hot and calm summer days (dog days)*

- Try an orange lure (Dog Nobbler) retrieved fast in the top six inches of water.
- Try a Coachman: sink and draw at various depths.
- Try a small, dry Welsh Partridge.
- Or sink and draw a Chomper on a floating line. Watch for takes on sink as well as draw.
- On a hot, still August or September afternoon cast out a Daddy Long Legs and leave it motionless to tempt trout.
- If there are occasional rises to sporadic midge hatches, try a leaded Shrimper. Cast it out and let it splash. Allow it to sink for a few seconds then draw it back a yard. If there is no take, repeat the tug. Keep the line tight

because the strike must be quick since a trout will reject it almost immediately. The trout cruising high in the water has a limited field of vision because of its height and it is attracted by the plop as the Shrimper hits the water.

- For tips about caenis, see 'Insect Identification and Behaviour' table on pages 71–87.

## Water conditions

*Algae or coloured water*

- Sink and draw an Aylott's Orange, especially, if possible, around the edge of the algae.

*Muddy water*

- Draw a black lure slowly through the muddy areas.

# General tips

- Check you have everything before leaving home using the checklist on page 96.
- Use checklist again when you pack up, especially in the dark, to avoid losses.
- Transport rods in a protective tube.
- Carry rods butt to the front in case you stumble; the rubber butt will take the shock.

## Leaders

- When fishing a dry fly, remember to degrease the last foot or so of the leader to prevent the nylon glinting next to the fly.
- Unless using suspenders, degrease the whole leader when fishing teams of nymphs so it will enter the water easily.
- As well as creating less wake, 'knotless' braided leaders are strong and do not get caught in the rod's eyes.
- Always carry a torch and casts with flies already attached if a late rise is expected.
- Check knots and the hook's barb after catching a fish or snagging the bottom.

## Boats

- Keep feet still.
- Keep everything tidy to prevent line snagging on bags, oars etc.
- If you do not row well, take a couple of elastic luggage straps to lash oars in rowlocks.

## Safety

- Take care walking when behind the casting arm of another angler.
- Wear eye protection and a hat, and boots with soles that grip.

- Only wade where it is safe. Check the area for potholes and ledges first.
- Wear a life-jacket when in a boat, wading or on precarious banks above deep water.
- Learn to cast with both hands so you can cast whichever way the wind blows.
- Use midge repellent cream – you can become sensitised.

## Finding fish

Fish and their location are effected by many factors: wind, temperature, food etc. but well-known holding areas include:

- The bank towards which the wind is or was blowing.
- In reservoirs, where old hedgerows, walls etc. run down into water.
- Where streams enter the lake.
- Off headlands jutting into deeper water.
- Wind lanes.
- Dam walls.
- Sainsbury's.

# Checklist

## DON'T FORGET IT!
### AND CHECK IT'S THE RIGHT ONE ...

ROD(S)
LANDING NET

**BAG**
REEL(S)

LINE(S) – Floating
      Sinking
LEADERS
CASTS
EXTRA MONOFILAMENT
FLIES & BOX – See
    *Monthly Guide*
FLY-FLOTANT
LINE SINK
PRIEST
BASS
TORCH
SCISSORS
PENKNIFE
CARBORUNDUM STONE
SNACK & DRINKS

FISHING PERMIT
ROD LICENCE
WALLET/MONEY

LIFE-JACKET
EYE PROTECTION
HAT
WADERS
BOOTS
WET WEATHER GEAR
TOWEL

HOUSE KEYS
CAR KEYS
PETROL
MAP
MOBILE PHONE – to leave in
                   car

**THESE SPACES ARE FOR YOU
TO ADD YOUR PERSONAL
REQUIREMENTS**

and the
***T & B
Fly Swotter***

**TELL SOMEONE WHERE YOU'RE GOING AND WHEN
YOU EXPECT TO BE BACK**